INTERNET WEALTH SECRETS

HOW TO MAKE MONEY ONLINE

ANTHONY EKANEM

Contents

Preface

The very first question you may ask is "why the Internet?" Well, this book will explain to you why this is the most profitable and hassle-free business in this time and age. You will be shown the several facts and figures to elaborate on the tremendous earning potential of Internet businesses. Let's look at the advantages of Internet business.

The Internet has been increasing that it becomes a primary tool for people to look for information! Simple as it might appear! Some categories of information, such as overweight, male impotence, debt, getting rich, MLM, etc., are considered to be so sensitive that people would not discuss with their folks offline. They'd instead go online and search because they know the virtual world will protect their identity and save them from shame. In other words, *the Internet is the place for people to look for solutions to their problems*. If you know how to target specific groups of people who are willing to spend on those solutions, you've made it!

Potential Growth in Value

I want to emphasize that more and more people are spending their money on the Internet. Nielsen reveals that 875 million consumers shopped online in 2008, and the trend is increasing rapidly. Now, with the popularity of Internet-connected mobile devices, people can spend money with just a click of a button. According to a study by the University of Oxford, there are more mobile subscribers than toothbrushes. So you can imagine how huge the market is and why you should tap onto this business as soon as possible before other millions of people come in and make it more difficult to monetize.

Flexibility

The Internet business gives you flexibility in working. You can choose to work at any time of the day, any day of the year, anywhere you prefer, as long as you have a computer and Internet connection. Your online store is the 24-hour salesman that continuously works for you even when you sleep.

Scalability

Internet business is a global business. You can sell to customers in Brazil, South Africa and India etc. without seeing them physically or setting up physical offices in those countries. It gives you a higher base of customer compared to a local business.

Small Start-up Cost

Let's do some cost analysis to compare an online business startup and a traditional brick-and-mortar business startup. The table below shows that Internet business is so affordable that even an average person can get started easily. If you want to startup offline, it would **cost you at least 1,000 times** more.

More and more people are planning to go online now. So, you'd better start soon so that you can still gain the early-mover advantage in the industry.

Cost of Starting A Business
Traditional business Internet business
Setup cost $300,000 Website setup $200
Rental fee $15,000 Hosting $7
Inventory cost $30,000 Software $20
Labour cost $20,000 Autoresponder $19
Utilities & others $10,000 PLR products $27
TOTAL $375,000 TOTAL $273

If you want to minimize your startup cost from the table above, you can! Let me give you a couple of examples:

If you can design a website yourself or outsource it to a cheap but quality service provider, you will cut your cost down even further. My very first website was built from a private label right (PLR) template that I purchased for less than $10, and it is now still up and running. You don't need to invest in an autoresponder service at the beginning stage. You can start small, and get it during the latter stage of your business as it grows bigger.

You don't need to buy PLR products if you can create an information product on your own.

You don't need a domain name or web hosting if you choose to build your website on a free platform such as Blogger or WordPress.

Small Maintenance Cost

Every month, you don't have to spend tens of thousands of dollars to maintain your business, just like this:

Monthly Cost of Running A Business
Traditional business Internet business
Rental fee $15,000 Hosting $7
Inventory cost $30,000 App & software $15
Labour cost $20,000 Autoresponder $19
Utilities $10,000 Website $50
Maintenance $2,000 Adwords $100
Marketing $20,000
TOTAL $97,000 TOTAL $191

You can cut cost for your Internet business if your budget is tight. For example, no hosting, no autoresponder, no Google Adwords campaigns etc.

Does it sound good to you? If yes, let's go straight into the and reveal the secrets right now. Just follow me; I am walking you through the **three profit centres** that guarantee to generate high returns on investments (by investment, I mean either money or time, or both).

CHAPTER ONE

Affiliate Marketing

Affiliate marketing is selling and promoting other people's products and services in return for a sales commission. This business model has become popular over the past few years, and it has created additional sources of income for hundreds of thousands of people around the world. Affiliate marketing creates a win-win-win situation, in which:

- The customers win because they have their problems solved
- The merchants (or vendors) win because they make money from the sales
- The affiliates win because they make money from the commissions, and don't have to own a product

Affiliate Marketing: A Closer Look

Let's look at one scenario to see the power of affiliate marketing. If a vendor sells a product at $47, and he can make 100 sales per month from his marketing effort, his total revenue is $47 x 100 = $4,700.

If he can get ten other affiliates (or joint venture partners) to promote his product and pays 75% commission for each sale made, and each affiliate can make

50 sales per month, what is the vendor's revenue? In this case, the vendor will be able to make 50 x 10 = 500 sales per month and generate a revenue of $47 x 500 = $23,500. He pays out 75% commission: 75% x $23,500 = $17,625 At the end of the day, the amount of money he put in his bank account is $23,500 – $17,625 = **$5,875.**

Wow, this is $1,175 more than his initial marketing effort without the help of the affiliates. And guess what, in this case, he earns money without any sales effort from his end! There you see the win-win-win situation! Is that the best scenario? No, because somebody can still gain a bigger slice in this case.

What if the vendor only gives out 60% of the revenue as commission, or just 50%, or even 35%? Sure he will make even more than $5,875 (if he has the same number of joint venture partners). What if he has 30 affiliates to promote his products instead of 10? I don't see how he can earn less than $5,875.

If the merchant has backend upsales for his product, the affiliates will earn commissions from the upsales as well. If the merchant offers a product or service with recurring payment, the affiliates will receive commissions on the recurring income too, as long as their customers don't cancel the subscription. That is why affiliate marketing has become so popular!

Affiliate Marketing Models

There are four common models of affiliate marketing:

- Pay Per Sale (PPS): You earn a commission for a product purchased or service rendered.
- Cost Per Action (CPA): You earn a commission when somebody completes specific action (such as filling in a form, completing a survey, etc.).

- Cost Per Click (CPC): You earn a commission when somebody clicks on an ad.
- Pay Per Install (PPI): You earn a commission when somebody install a software or application on their computer.

The Myths of Affiliate Marketing

You may ask: "If everybody is doing affiliate marketing, how can I profit from it?" Simple! The online marketplace is just a simulation of its offline counterpart, in which there are demands and supplies for products or services in thousands of different niches. Different people will look for different things to buy. For instance, rich people are looking for high-end luxury sports cars.

Many youngsters spend money buying condoms and sex toys. Overweight individuals are looking for weight loss solutions. Low-income workers look for opportunities to earn extra income from home. Retired people consume travel services. You name it! So, you don't need to worry about doing something that everybody is doing, and getting nothing out of it. The chances are that you will be able to find profitable niches with moderate competition to start making money. The only issue is whether you are decisive enough to take the early-mover advantage.

You may also wonder whether affiliate marketing is a form of multi-level marketing (MLM)? The answer is NO!!! In affiliate marketing, you are a salesperson, promoting products or services to those who need them and earn a commission from the sales you make.

Unlike most MLM programs, you don't have to buy any product before being accepted into an affiliate program. However, you should try the product first to understand it better and promote it more effectively. In affiliate marketing, you are not recruiting downlines, and your customers don't have to recruit their downlines either. You may retain a customer in your list and resell to them in the future. This is not the same as the MLM model.

The Affiliate Marketer Roadmap

Step #1: Market Research

If you want to sell something, you need to make sure that somebody out there is willing to buy it. This is called "finding the hungry crowds" who will spend their money on the products you are promoting.

The fastest way to make money is to understand the problems that many people are seeking solutions to. Only in these cases are people willing to take out their credit card and make a purchase. Below are some examples of common problems people always try to solve:

- Weight loss
- Real estate
- Dog training
- Make money online
- Dating solutions
- Men impotence
- Investment solutions
- etc.

There are several ways of doing market research:

- You can go to **Google Hot Trend** to find out what are the things people are crazy about during a specific period, and what are they willing to spend money on. (http://www.google.com/trends/)

- You can go to **eHow.com** to find out the problems that a majority of people are seeking solutions to.

- You can visit **43Things.com** to find out what many people want to do.

- **Amazon (http://www.amazon.com/)** is another place because it lets you know what products are selling well. Simply visit the website, go to Features & Services, Amazon Exclusive, Amazon Bestseller to acquire the updated buying trend and behaviour.

- **Clickbank (http://www.clickbank.com/)** is the largest online marketplace for digital products. I'll explain more about how it works in the upcoming appendix in this section.

- Alternatively, you can find tons and tons of information on relevant blogs and forums.

Step #2: Decide A Niche

Once you have done your market research, you can choose a niche to go into. My advice is that you choose only ONE solid niche first and work on it until you make some money out of it. Don't try multi-niches when you just get started because it won't give you any reliable result.

I am currently working on only four niches, and these have been my decent streams of income months after months.

You can do some research and consider these following niches:

- Dog training

- Golf techniques
- Dating solutions
- FOREX investment training and software
- Gardening
- Body-building
- You name it!

Step #3: Find A Product To Promote

There are many places out there where you can find a product to promote. Most of them are free and easy to use.

Commission Junction

One of the biggest affiliate marketplaces is **Commission Junction (http://www.cj.com/)**, which is also the pioneer network in the affiliate marketing landscape. Here, you can find any high-quality products to promote, ranging from physical to digital, paying good commission. Their affiliate programmes also provide you with useful tools and support so that you won't get lost during your partnership with them. You can go ahead and sign up as a publisher to start promoting products on CJ right now!

Market Health

Market Health (http://www.markethealth.com/) is a perfect place if you are in the health and beauty niche. This network allows you to market and promote the world's leading health and beauty offers online. They offer high paying affiliate programmes and good tracking software in the industry. Offers include products in the health, beauty, supplement, weight loss, and skincare industries.

This affiliate network has many commission options for affiliates, including both a revenue share and flat CPA, and the opportunity to make residual recurring income on customers. You can direct your prospects to a landing page that offers a free trial product. If the customers come back and order more in the future, you take the credit. Market Health also provides a second-tier commission scheme. This scheme allows you to earn on the sales referred by your customers. This might sound like MLM's downline structure, but the natures of the two models are different.

Amazon

Amazon also offers its affiliate program, known as Amazon associate program. Coming across as the world's largest online retailer, Amazon offers a wide range of products from books, electronic devices, jewellery, toys to consumer goods. The company reported its revenue to be $48 billion in 2011. Amazon pays a commission ranging from 4% to 15% to affiliates who promote the products listed on their website. Amazon has retail sites for many countries around the world, including the US, Canada, the UK, France, Germany, Italy, Spain, Japan, and China. The company is also expected to launch its websites in Poland, Netherlands and Sweden.

Clickbank

Suppose you want to promote instantly downloadable digital products with high commission rate, head over to **Clickbank** now. This the largest digital product marketplace, with over 100,000 active affiliate marketers promoting more than 46,000 individual products, processing 35,000 transactions per day and generating over $350,000,000 in revenue in 2011. Clickbank products are available for over 200 countries worldwide. In Clickbank, you can find products of many niches, from those as popular as Internet marketing, weight loss, gardening, to less popular such as languages, martial arts etc. When you promote Clickbank products, the maximum commission rate you can enjoy is 75%. I have prepared a case study below to give you a closer look at this wonderful marketplace.

Google Adsense

Google Adsense offers a Cost Per Click affiliate scheme. It allows you to display Google ads on your blogs/ websites. Every time people click on the ads, you will make money.

To be accepted into the Google Adsense program, you will need to build a blog or website with good and acceptable contents. Google will only accept copyrighted materials on your blog/ website. Below are unacceptable contents or links to those contents:

- Pornography, adult or mature content
- Violent content
- Content related to racial intolerance or advocacy against any individual, group or organization
- Excessive profanity
- Hacking/cracking content
- Gambling or casino-related content
- Illicit drugs and drug paraphernalia content
- Sales of beer or hard alcohol
- Sales of tobacco or tobacco-related products
- Sales of prescription drugs
- Sales of weapons or ammunition (e.g. firearms, firearm components, fighting knives, stun guns)
- Sales of products that are replicas or imitations of designer or other goods
- Sales or distribution of coursework or student essays
- Content regarding programs which compensate users for clicking ads or offers, performing searches, surfing websites or reading emails
- Any other illegal content promotes illegal activity or infringes on the legal rights of others

The allowed percentage of repeated keyword is only at 3-4% of your content. Google is strict on its policy. If it discovers any violation from your side, your account will be immediately suspended.

CPA Programmes

CPA is usually referred to as a "high-end" affiliate programme because it offers many attractive schemes that pay good commissions. As introduced earlier, you don't need to make a sale to earn a commission. All you need to do is getting people to click on your affiliate link, fill in a form, complete a survey, register for a trial product or download something to their computers and your commission is recognized.

With that in mind, I have to highlight to you that it is not easy to be accepted into these CPA programmes unless you are experienced in Internet marketing. The CPA network will call you up for a phone interview when they receive your application. Based on the conversation, they will decide whether to accept you as their CPA partner.

Below are some popular CPA networks:

- Neverblue (**http://www.neverblue.com/**)
- Maxbounty (**http://maxbounty.com/**)
- Share A Sale (http://shareasale.com/)

Step #4: Keyword Research

Studying consumer behaviour is a vital part of any marketing process. In Internet marketing, this is referred to as 'keyword research'. One of the most powerful and free resources to conduct keyword research is **Google Keywords Tool** (**https://adwords.google.com/o/ KeywordTool/**).

You can create a free account and start researching for keyword any time you are ready. This tool lets you know how many people are searching for a particular keyword and how competitive it is on the market. Keyword research is the key to your success on the Internet. Many Internet marketers don't do keyword research, and they end up earning nothing and giving up. So if you want to stand out from the crowd, you should do it. It's not difficult to do, and what is more, it's free!!! Just head towards Google Keyword Tool, type in the keyword that is relevant to the niche you selected. It will display a list of related keywords for you.

Next, you need to pick up five keywords to target, preferably longtail keywords, something like "how to lose belly fat". The keyword should have more than 1,000 global searches per month and less than 10,000 competing sites. Your keywords will be a powerful weapon for most of your promotional activities later on.

Step #5: Create Your Landing Page

A landing page can be:

- The sales page of the vendor.
- A presales page linking to the vendor's sales page.
- A blog with product reviews and links to the vendor's sales page.
- A squeeze page, to capture visitors' email address and build a list for yourself.

Just give me a moment to talk about building a list with a squeeze page. Maybe you are not interested in it right now at the beginning stage. But as you move forward, you will realize that this is the ultimate affiliate marketing method of all time. Research shows that more than 95% of the traffic coming to a website will just leave without buying anything. That is why we need to convert these visitors into buying customers over time slowly. You need to collect their email addresses for future follow-ups. The list is the most valuable asset that Internet marketers will ever want to possess, simply because the money is in the list. The list is your instant ATM, as long as you know how to use it properly.

Step #6: Drive Traffic to Your Landing Page

Whatever your landing page is, you need the traffic to make money. As gurus always say, traffic is the lifeblood of internet business. Without traffic, you won't be able to make a dime. There are many free techniques to drive traffic to your landing page. I am going to share with you some effective methods to drive quality traffic to your website:

Method #1: Classified Ads

There are many free classified ads websites out there, but the best is **Craigslist (http://craigslist.org/)**. Craigslist is built around communities, with localized sites for 450 cities worldwide.

Average monthly page views of this website amount to over 9 billion, with traffic sources from all parts of the world. This is such a great website that eBay has thrown out its money to acquire 25% of the equity in Craigslist. You will see how great it is when you start using it for your business. Over 80% of the Craigslist audience is from 18 to 49 years old. Here you will find some ad categories that are relevant to different niches and products. When posting on classified ad sites, you need to understand the rules of those sites to avoid your account being suspended due to violation.

Craigslist gives you access to global traffic! Tips for posting classified ads: teaser style, short and sweet, straight to the point, with attractive headlines. Don't post a long sales letter there or nobody is going to read it.

Other classified ads services you can register to include:

- ClassifiedAds.com
- USFreeAds.com
- AdLandPro.com
- INetGiant.com

They are all FREE to use!

Method #2: Article Submission

The concept of using articles is similar to that of creating a free product. An article is a free information source that web surfers are keen to explore. A well-written article earns you major credibility points. It enhances your expertise in the eyes of your potential customers.

It also drives tons of traffic and creates quality backlinks to your landing page and pulls it up in the search engine listings. The most popular article directory is **Ezine Articles.** It has millions of quality contents on almost every topic. On average, over 2,000,000 visitors to this site are from the US every single month.

If you own a good piece of content, people can pull it out to place on their blogs. Other article directories also retrieve high-quality contents from Ezine Articles and post them back on their sites. This enhances the backlinks to the content owner's website. People always say: content is king! Great content will last for a long time. It will spread all over the Internet to bring unlimited traffic to the webmaster.

So, what do you need to do now?

- Register an account at Ezine Articles.

- Produce a couple of good contents related to what you are promoting.
- Remember to use the keywords in the title, the introduction, throughout the article and the tag box.
- Post your content
- Keyword density: Only 2-5% of the whole article.
- Post your author information in the resource box, with a link to your landing page.

Remember to check the terms and conditions before you post your first article on this directory. By the way, you don't need to be a good writer to produce good content. You can extract information on other sources over the Internet and modify it into your unique article. You can also outsource the writing at Elance or Fiverr at low cost, or use PLR articles. Just remember not to copy and paste plainly and, more importantly, make sure to include your keyword in the articles. After your article is approved and published on Ezine Articles, you can go ahead and post it on your blog and other article directories to multiply incoming traffic.

Below are some popular article directories that you can consider:

- ArticleBase.com
- GoArticles.com
- ArticleAlley.com
- Amazines.com

Method #3: Yahoo! Answers
Yahoo! Answers is an online community where you can post questions and answer people's questions to help them solve their problems. You can quote the link to your landing

page as the source of information you are referring to in your answer. Just make sure that it is not an affiliate link. Otherwise, your account will be suspended. If people find your answers great and relevant, they will contact you for more information, and you can pick up from there for your direct promotion. If your answer is rated to be the best, the chances are that many people will continue to see it over time when they search for the questions. This is real and solid traffic! Again, you should browse through the terms and conditions to understand what Yahoo! likes and what it doesn't.

Method #4: Press Releases

An online press release is simply a traditional press release that is distributed through online channels. This is a fantastic way to create buzz, increase online visibility, and drive website traffic through inbound links to your website. Writing a press release is different from writing an article. It has its format and writing style. The beauty of press release is search engines love them!

Components of a press release include:

- Title/ Headline
- Subtitle
- Introduction
- Body
- Company bio
- Ending
- Contact information

Below are some basic press release guidelines:

1. The information you present must be newsworthy. You don't want your press release to sound like an advertisement, but it's fine to announce your web presence

or the launch of a new product. A good press release should be informative only, and not a sales pitch. The object of the press release is to provide specific information regarding your particular business, product, or site.

2. Target your readers: The audience, when reading your release, should understand why this information is relevant to them. Give them a reason to keep reading.

3. Use the best possible lead-in headline you can come up with. Then, keep it simple, incorporate the headline into the first sentence of the main body of the press release.

4. Make it clear who you are. Always lead with the announcement, and follow with the source.

5. Your copy should help the reader connect and relate. Explain "why", "how", "when" and "where". Include a benefit.

6. Write in an objective tone of voice. You can convey import or excitement, but avoid using too many adjectives or fancy language. Stay focused on facts.

7. Make sure you include as much contact information as possible. This means The name of the person to contact regarding the press release, a phone number, fax, snail mail address if applicable, email address and website address.

8. Check your press release over several times. Have a friend or relative proof-read it as well. Correct spelling mistakes. Make sure your release offers something of substance.

Below are some free press release distribution services that you can leverage on:

- PRLog.org
- I-Newswire.com
- Free-Press-Release.com
- PR.com

Method #5: Video Marketing

People love videos. Search engines love videos. That's why video marketing is considered as the massive traffic generation tool. This is a high converting method, but it is still underused at this point. As of now, the most popular video-sharing platform is **Youtube.**

Founded in 2005, Youtube has now become the most visited video-sharing website over the Internet, attracting more than 2 billion views every single day. It reaches over 81 million US viewers monthly. Youtube was bought over by Google at $1.65 billion in 2006.

Let me share with you some interesting statistics about Youtube:

- An average viewer spends at least 15 minutes per day on Youtube
- 70% of all Youtube traffic comes from outside of the US
- Youtube is localized in 23 countries, with 24 different languages
- More videos are uploaded on Youtube in 60 days than the combine efforts of all three major US networks in 60 years
- Youtube videos are embedded in tens of millions of other websites over the Internet

(Source: viralblog.com)

How can you tap on this powerful platform to drive massive traffic to your website?

- Create a video related to your niche. Again, you can outsource or use PLR materials.
- Post the video on Youtube, with keywords in the video file name, video title, description and tag.

- Put your website URL in the description box.
- It is even better if you can create a clickable overlay on the video that links to your website.

Besides, you can submit your files to other video sharing platforms to multiply traffic to your landing page. Below are some quality websites:

- TubeMogul.com
- Veoh.com
- Metacafe.com
- Dailymotion.com

Method #6: Forum Participation

Online forums are the places where people hang around every day to search and share information. On forums, you will get a chance to interact with many real and new people every day.

I'm going to show you how to start forum marketing effectively:

1) Searching for popular forums relating to your niche (on Google or ForumFind.com).

2) Joining the forum and saying hi in the welcome room so that people notice that you have just joined.

3) Including your website URL in your profile.

4) Actively participating in the forum to get rapport with people, also to learn from others about the topic you are promoting.

5) Up to a certain point of time, including the link to your landing page in your signature.

Again, you should understand the rules of the forums to avoid account suspension. This method needs a little bit of hard work, but it significantly pays off eventually. You will not only increase traffic to your site but also convert and retain some customers as well as enhance your branding!

Moreover, as I mentioned, participating in forums is one of the best ways to improve your knowledge and expertise in the niches you are promoting. One golden rule about forum marketing: Never post affiliate links anywhere in any forums! Most forum moderators hate that.

Method #7: Social Networks

Currently, **Facebook** (http://www.facebook.com/) and **Twitter** (http://twitter.com/) are the most popular social media websites on the Internet. They provide excellent interactive platforms for their users.

These are the great sources of viral traffic, and it's a waste of resources if you miss out these channels. Besides, you can also tap on to **LinkedIn** (http://www.linkedin.com/) to approach the professional segment, especially if you are in the investment and Internet business niches.

Coming up next, we are witnessing the rapid growth of **Google+**. This could be a great platform because it is owned by Google and will be loved by Google search engine. **Squidoo** (http://www.squidoo.com) and **HubPages** (http://hubpages.com/) are search engines' favourite platforms and traffic attraction hubs day in day out. On these two platforms, you can post a series of quality contents related to your niche to share information and promote your affiliate products. Again, don't forget your keywords!

Method #8: Social Bookmark

Social bookmarking sites, also known as content aggregators, allow users to submit and share their favourite URLs. They also allow members to vote for their favourite links. Social bookmarking is all about information sharing. If your URL receives votes from other users, it will receive greater visibility from the search engines and web surfers.

That's why social bookmarking has become such an essential component of Internet marketing that nobody should ever ignore the power of it. There are many social bookmarking websites out there. Below are the best places to get started:

- OnlyWire.com
- Digg.com
- Delicious.com
- StumbleUpon.com
- Reddit.com

Method #9: Document Sharing

When this method was first invented, people just considered it as a platform to share and distribute documents over the Internet. Now it has gone beyond that function and become a powerful platform for Internet marketers to drive viral traffic to their sites. Document sharing websites allow users to share their files in DOC, PDF, PPT and many other formats. Most of the files uploaded will be visible and downloadable by the public unless an author chooses to privatize his files. Usually, marketers will embed hyperlinks to their landing page or affiliate offers in the documents.

If you want to create a good document to attract a significant amount of views, pay attention to the following components:

- Attractive title
- Nicely structured content
- High converting visual aids
- Relevant keywords
- Good author profile

This method is, in fact, still underused at this moment in time. You can make use of it once you get started. Here are some authority document sharing sites that are loved by the search engines:

- SlideShare.net
- Slide.com
- Scribd.com
- Calameo.com

As an affiliate marketer, you should take note of the following:

- Trust building is essential. Don't let consumers think of you as a scammer. You need to be sincere in the way you communicate, and turn up as a knowledgeable or experienced person in the niche you are promoting. If you are not an expert yet, you can pick it up fast during your promotional activities that I introduced above.

- Don't promote any products that come along your way. Only promote good products. Many marketers make this mistake and ruin their branding; so I just want to make sure that you are on the right track.

- Give customers what they want. Don't promote irrelevant pieces of stuff or you will be blacklisted. People will buy from you if they trust you. If they buy from you once, there is a high chance that they will return and buy from you again in the future. But if you create a wrong impression, they will say farewell to you!

- Don't promote products that are too competitive. Be a small fish in the big pond is always the best strategy.

- Most importantly, remember NOT TO SPAM!

CHAPTER TWO

Using eBay

People come to eBay by the millions. Thus, eBay is so far the world's largest online auction company and one of the highest traffic attractions on the Internet. The company's revenue was up to $10.77 billion in 2010. And it is the Top 21 most visited website at the time of this writing. You can find almost everything that you'd want to purchase on eBay, from used cars to a pepper grinder made from a stuffed raccoon.

eBay has become the world's largest and most diversified marketplace. From high class and high priced to trailer trash chic selling for pennies, anything you want is at your fingertips. eBay is the owner of **PayPal**, the world's largest digital payment solution provider.

How to Monetize with eBay

1) Selling Your Own Products

It can be anything in the house that you don't want anymore. It can be something that you buy at a low price from the pawnshop. Just make sure that you don't make a loss on your trade. I have seen many people waiting for super sales periods such as Black Friday sales in the US. They will invest in cheap stuff and resell it on eBay one or two months later. You can also sell your information products on eBay if you are an infopreneur.

2) Selling Other People's Products

You can sign up for the eBay Partner Network and promoting the products there for commission. Make use of all the techniques shared above if you choose to go this way.

3) Dropshipping

This is a more advanced method and a profitable business. In this model, your role is the same as an affiliate marketer. The only difference is that the payment is made to you, not to the vendor. And you are the one who decides how much profit you would like to make.

You need to post an ad on eBay (or any other platforms). When you receive an order from your customer, you notify the vendors (also known as the drop shipper), and they will handle all the shipping and delivery for you. You receive the money from the customer, pay it to the vendor and keep the profit. Dropshipping deals with physical products. To find products to promote, you simply need to visit the **Wholesale Central (http://www.wholesalecentral.com/)** and view the listing there. After selecting your product, you can create your listing on eBay.

Dropshipping is a good business model because it:

- Minimizes the risk of inventory obsolescence, because you don't need to store inventory at all.
- Eliminates the costs of shipping and handling and from your side.
- Offers convenience, no physical logistics actions required.
- Provides practicality and ability to sell different products at the same time.
- Generates high profits with seasonal purchasing patterns.

All in all, eBay is a great place to do business. Do it the right way, and you will make a fortune out of it. Let me share with you some useful tips to do business on eBay:

- Conduct market research to know the buying trends so that you can pick the profitable products to promote. Collect useful information for your analysis at **eBay Pulse** (http://pulse.ebay.com/).

- Always use great pictures when listing a product. Don't leave it blank or competitors will grab your customers. Great visual aids always attract buyers!

- Use **PayPal** as a mode of payment. (Remember? eBay owns PayPal).

- Run the auction for at least seven days, extend it after it expires. The longer your ads is live, the more leads it can capture.

CHAPTER THREE

Information Products

In this time and age, information is money, and those who sell information can easily laugh their ways to the bank. The history of Internet marketing has witnessed many self-made millionaires, just from selling information products. And I called them infopreneurs. The beauty of selling information products is that you can earn passive income months after months, even years after years.

Information Product Deliveries

There are many ways to monetize on a piece of information product, both online and offline. Below are some common examples:

1. Normal delivery

- Physical book (offline)
- Ebook for PC (online)
- Ebook for Kindle, NOOK, iPad etc. (offline)
- Private label rights and master resell rights (online)
- E-newsletter (online)
- Membership subscription (online)

2. Interactive delivery

- Audiobook (online)

- Training video series (online)
- CD and DVD (offline)
- Workshop (offline & online)
- Seminar (offline)
- Webinar (online)

The Beauty of Info Business

To be a successful infopreneur doesn't mean you have to be an expert in a particular field. You don't need to be an expert to start creating and selling information products. You just need an interest and enthusiasm in the topic. That is more than enough.

Selling information product doesn't require you to bear inventory and delivery cost because your information product is stored in digital form and can be downloaded by your customers right after they send you the payment. Your profit margin is 100%. Your digital information product is a great tool to up-sell or cross-sell other products, whether yours or others' in the form of affiliate links.

Last but not least, the demand for information products has increased significantly over the years. People are spending big money online and offline to buy books, ebooks, training courses and consultation services to solve their problems. (sounds familiar, right?)

Creating Your Information Products

As an infopreneur, your starting point is almost the same as an affiliate marketer. You need to select your topic (or niche) before you can start creating your information products. The topic you choose can be something that you are passionate about, such as golf, gardening, music; or it can be any problem that many people are facing and trying to find solutions to. Now you've got a chance to recycle the same niche and keyword research techniques in the income path #1.

Let's get started to create your information products.

1. **Using Information from the Internet**

The Internet is an affluent resource of information. You can find both reliable and unreliable contents about almost everything. If you want to create high-quality information products, you need to filter the sources and pick up the most reliable and solid materials for your information products.

There are many great resources for you to refer to. I often go to these following places to extract information:

- Wikipedia
- Ezine Articles directory
- Blogs and Forums
- eHow.com
- Documents sharing websites
- Publications by universities, institutions and government authorities

If you collect the information this way, bear in mind the following principles:

- Don't copy and paste plainly or you will be sued for copyright infringement. Paraphrase the materials to make your contents unique!
- Credit to the content owners whenever possible.
- Filter the information carefully to avoid junk information.

2) Using MRR and PLR Materials

Now, it's time to discuss the important concepts that I keep mentioning so far throughout this book: Master Resell Rights (MRR) and Private Label Rights (PLR). Without these items, the Internet marketing landscape would have been so different from what it is today! And I am sure that without them, many newbies would struggle to start their online business.

Four basics rights are prevailing all over the virtual world:

- Unrestricted Private Label Rights
- Private Label Rights
- Master Resell Rights
- Resell Rights

Unrestricted Private Label Rights: This is the most flexible of all rights and thus, most valuable. You can do almost everything with free PLR products (renaming, branding and selling as your own, editing, and bundling with other products in a package). You can also give them away, and you can sell or give away the rights for others to resell, master resell, or private label it.

Private Label Rights (PLR): Similarly, with this right, you can rewrite, edit, and claim to yourself to be the creator. But usually, they have some limitations such as price floor and restrictions of giveaway right.

Master Resell Rights (MRR): This right allows you to resell products but not edit them in any way. You cannot put your name as the author of the product as well. Nor can you add or edit the content in any manners. With Master Resell Rights, you can also sell or give away the resell rights to others, and often you can give away the Master Resell Rights, allowing others to resell the resell rights.

Resell Rights: This is the weakest of all rights and therefore, the least valuable. You can only resell the product. You cannot change it in any way, and you cannot give away or sell the resell rights either.

A PLR/MRR contract (or terms & conditions) will look like this:

[YES] Can be edited

[YES] Can put your name as the author.

[YES] Can be broken down into articles.

[YES] Can be used as web or ezine content.

[YES] Can be added to membership websites.

[YES] Can be sold in any format.

[YES] Can be packaged.

[YES] Can be offered as a bonus.

[YES] Can be given away (in any format).

[NO] Can be sold on auction sites.

[NO] Can offer (Master) Resell Rights

[NO] Can resell Private Label Rights.

[YES] Can be published offline.

To find high-quality PLR/MRR materials, I recommend you to these following two websites:

1.   The   Warrior   Forum (http://www.warriorforum.com/)

2. Resale Superstore (http://master-resale-rights.com/)

3) Using Public Domain Works

Public domain works are products whose copyright has expired. You can recycle the public domain materials and modify them into your information product, then re-copyright and sell it. The largest public domain resource on the Internet is **Gutenberg.org**.

4) Hiring A Ghost Writer

In the economics perspective, outsourcing is always the optimal solution to your business because it saves you time to fully specialize in your core competencies and maximize your business outcome.

If you are not strong in writing, and you are willing to spend some money, then outsourcing is an excellent option for you. There are bunches of hungry and skilful ghostwriters out there. They are superb at writing but not marketing. That's why most of them focus fully on writing, and the Internet marketers are those who monetize on their works. Why do we call these people ghostwriters? Simply because we don't know who they are, and may never have a chance to see them in person... until we all become ghosts!!! (Well, just kidding over here!).

You can find many good writers on **Elance**, who are equipped with full resume, track records and client ratings. Besides, you can also visit **Fiverr** and hire someone to do the work for you for only $5. Similar to Elance, Fiverr allows you to view the full ratings of the service providers so that you can make a better decision. By the way, this book is not written by a ghostwriter.

Well, I hope this has given you a better idea of how to start your infopreneur journey. I can tell you that this business is enormous and growing.

Selling Your Information Product

Before distributing your information product, I recommend you register for a PayPal account. This is the most convenient electronic payment solutions nowadays. You can sign up for a personal account with Paypal. Along the way, while you are growing your Internet business, you can start upgrading to a premier or business account. You can sell your information products through three main channels as demonstrated on the earlier infopreneur roadmap. I am going to explain a little more in details how each channel works.

Selling Your Information Products Online

There are various ways to sell your products online. For a start, you can concentrate on these following two methods:

1) eBay listings

You can list your information products on eBay, create a PayPal "Pay Now" button, upload your product to the Internet, and give customers the download link after they make payments.

You can upload your information products to:

- Your website
- A WordPress blog
- Free sharing services: YouSendIt, MediaFire etc.

There are three tricks for promoting and advertising your products on eBay. First, eBay auctions can be used as a test-bed for a new product before its official launch. You put your product up for auction and open bidding to start. The idea is to sell x number of copies until you determine the highest average price that customers are willing to pay for your product. This way, you not only get some vital data on pricing, but you also get something else: exposure.

Second, your "About Me" page is another great promotional tool. While eBay forbids linking out to other sites in your auctions, you can link to several external URLs of your choice in your profile.

Third, you can use eBay for list building. You'll have your customer's email address automatically when he pays you. So you can send him follow-up emails in the future when you launch new products.

2) Digital Product Marketplace

Earlier in this book, I have introduced Clickbank as the largest digital products' marketplace on the Internet. Now, we are revisiting it, because as an infopreneur, it is an excellent platform for you to sell your information products. When you sign up as an affiliate at Clickbank, by default, you can be a vendor yourself if you already have something to sell. Selling information products with Clickbank, you don't need to worry much about customer transaction and communication because Clickbank will do all the work for you. (Of course, you still have to respond to customer enquiries, but Clickbank makes it simple for you to do so).

If you own a great product, you don't need to worry much about marketing either. A big team of affiliates at Clickbank will be able to promote your products for you. You just need to get your product launched, then run a JV competition, and watch the affiliates promote your products.

However, Clickbank is quite a premium place to start with, especially If you have a budget constraint. You have to pay a listing fee of $50 to list your product on Clickbank, and the transaction fee is quite high for every sale you make. In this case, you can head over to **Click2Sell (http://www.click2sell.eu/)** to start distributing your products at no cost. You only pay transaction fees when you make a sale, and the rate is much lower than Clickbank. The only trade-off is that the affiliate base of these two networks is not as strong as Clickbank.

Selling MRR and PLR

If you can buy PRL products to create your articles or ebook, you can also sell your information products as MRR or PLR products. You can sell or giveaway MRR if your product contains a link to your landing page or affiliate offers, or if you simply want to build your brand and let many people know about you. You can sell PLR if you can write quick and decent contents in short periods.

PLR materials don't need to be superb quality products with beautiful graphics and layout, because people will still modify them anyway. Selling PLR is a very profitable business because not many people can write well and fast, and most of them need contents on the go. If you want to sell PLR, you have the option to protect your creator rights, such as imposing specific price restriction as an anti-dumping policy. Do refer to the sample PLR terms & conditions introduced earlier to come up with your own.

Publishing Information Products Offline

When you have a great piece of content, you can go ahead and publish your information products with major publishing houses or book retailers locally and globally. In this section, I'm going to reveal some convenient platforms for you to start publishing and selling your information products, especially books, offline.

1) Self-publishing services

There are two channels for you to self-publish your physical books.

- Kindle Direct Publishing (https://kdp.amazon.com)
- Lulu (http://www.lulu.com)

Kindle Direct Publishing is a platform owned by Amazon. It allows you to publish your contents at no cost, like physical books, CDs or DVDs, and distribute your contents on Amazon with no additional charge. If you pay upgrading fees, it can make your publications available to major online and offline retailers, libraries and academic institutions through the company's arrangement with

Ingram, Baker & Taylor. It can also make your books available directly to certified retailers through its wholesale website.

The Createspace platform provides you with step-by-step guidelines to publish your books, from registering for an ISBN, formatting your interior layout, designing your cover, pricing and distributing your books. Of course, if you have a budget, you can pay Createspace to do most of the steps for you. But it is interesting to find out how to do it yourself step by step. I enjoyed it when I first got started.

Another self-publishing company is called Lulu. The company has over 1.1 million creators from more than 200 countries and territories who sign up to publish their contents. Each month, Lulu adds approximately 20,000 titles to its catalogue. Similar to Createspace, it's free to publish at Lulu, and you can create everything from hardcover and paperback books to eBooks, photo books and calendars.

The company operates a global print network and provides worldwide distribution so that authors can reach readers from all over the world. Lulu expands its distribution networks to Amazon, Barnes & Nobles and many international book retailers. Lulu also provides expert assistance services for authors who have a budget. Its services range from cover design, editing, formatting and marketing.

2) Publishing ebooks for e-reader devices

Hooray... statistics time again! I love playing with numbers... At the time of this writing, the market share for mobile tablets is rising. And the trend of reading ebooks on these mobile devices is increasing significantly. According to research done by author Christopher Maselli, Amazon Kindle controls over 60% of the entire ebook market, and the number is rising. Apple iPad controls about 16% of the e-reader market, while Barnes & Nobles' Nook controls 20% of the market. You can see that Kindle is currently the market leader of this segment. Nielsen's research also revealed that 44% of Kindle users are high-income individuals who make more than $80,000 a year. 27% of them possess a Master's degree or PhD. Half of the Kindle owners worldwide are below 35 years old.

Los Angeles Times reveals that among hard-core readers who go through 25 books or more a year, 44% prefer using Kindle on the iPad. So, the point I want to make here is that e-reader book is a huge and fast-growing market, especially Kindle. A poll conducted by Harris Interactive in 2010, from the responses of 2,775 adults, indicates that while 19% of all Americans read 21 or more books a year, 26% of those who own e-readers read 21 or more books a year.

E-reader devices have transformed people's reading habit worldwide, and this opens a vast horizon for infopreneurs who would like to enter this lucrative market. Before showing you how to start, I would like to quote one more finding from AOL Daily Finance: One author who declared to have sold 6,315 titles through Amazon, only reported 16 copies in iBookstore sales.

Now, let's visit **Amazon Kindle**'s website at **https://kdp.amazon.com/** to create a free account and start publishing your information products. Do spend some time to read the publishing guidelines, especially the formatting and publishing process. Once you are ready to launch your very first product, just go ahead and do it step-by-step. It's really simple. Don't sell any MRR products there because Amazon hates to see duplicated contents on their bookstore.

After successfully publishing your book on Kindle, you can go back to Lulu to publish an ebook. Your ebook will be distributed to Barnes & Noble's Nook store and Apple's iBookstore. When publishing on Lulu, do not include any table in your source file. Take screenshots if you need to have tables.

Lulu will convert your ebook into epub format. You don't need to have a table of contents for epub files. It will automatically generate for you, as long as you format your documents with the following:

- Chapter headlines: Heading 1
- Section headlines: Heading 2
- Sub-section headline: Heading 3

And you are now ready to publish your contents! Fantastic! Isn't it? Once you have got all the books listed, just spend your effort in marketing them, and see the royalties flow in.

3) Publishing books offline

With a good piece of content, you can approach major publishing houses locally and globally to submit your manuscript for their reviews. Once your book is approved and published, you will start seeing passive income! One technique to earn more royalty every year is to keep updating your content so that the new edition of your book continues to sell well.

Again, you don't need to be an expert to become a best-seller. Robert Kiyosaki, the best-selling author of **Rich Dad, Poor Dad** once emphasized during an interview that he is not a bestselling author. However, his book still sells well because he knows how to target the audience and market his books properly. Who knows you might be the next best-selling author?

Conclusion

Does it seem too complicated to make money online? Well, it is much simpler than making money offline! I hope you enjoy reading this book. I believe it has provided you with the basic principles of Internet marketing for your future success.

Before we end, I would want to emphasize that Internet marketing is not a get-rich-quick scheme. As far as I observe, most of the get-rich-quick schemes promise to help you make money faster than you can imagine, and in the end, they run away with your money.

If you do it the right way, you will be able to stay away from the scammers and secure your decent stream of income online for the long-term.

To pave the way for your future success, you need to:

- Focus on what you are doing
- Avoid jumping from products to products, offers to offers, gurus to gurus, systems to systems, or you would never hit your target
- Be patient and willing to learn from both achievements and mistakes
- Follow the right instructions from the right people
- Keep upgrading yourself in the fast-changing environment
- Grasp the opportunity when it comes (as it may not reoccur) With that in mind, I am going to close this book here.